D0759149

D.J. and the JAZZ FEST

D.J. and the JAZZ FEST

Denise Walter McConduit

Illustrated by Emile F. Henriquez

PELICAN PUBLISHING COMPANY
Gretna 2004

Copyright © 1997
By Denise Walter McConduit
All rights reserved
First printing, February 1997
Second printing, February 2004

*In commemoration of the 100th anniversary of jazz,
and to my wonderful children, Crishelle, Monique, Erika, and D.J.
Thanks for being my inspiration. With love, Mother*

---

*The word "Pelican" and the depiction of a pelican are trademarks
of Pelican Publishing Company, Inc.,
and are registered in the U.S. Patent and Trademark Office.*

Library of Congress Cataloging-in-Publication Data

McConduit, Denise Walter.
    D.J. and the Jazz Fest / by Denise Walter McConduit ; illustrated
by Emile F. Henriquez.
        p.   cm.
    Summary: Although he does not want to go at first, D.J. has a good
time and learns a lot when he joins his mother and her godmother at
the annual jazz festival in New Orleans.
    ISBN 1-56554-239-8 (hc)
    1. New Orleans Jazz & Heritage Festival—Juvenile Fiction.
[1. New Orleans Jazz & Heritage Fesival—Fiction. 2. Jazz-
-Fiction. 3. New Orleans (La.)—Fiction. 4. Afro-Americans-
-Fiction.]   I. Henriquez, Emile F., ill. II. Title.
PZ7.M478414196Dab 1997
[E]—dc21
                                    96-46639
                                        CIP
                                        AC

Printed in China

Published by Pelican Publishing Company, Inc.
1000 Burmaster Street, Gretna, Louisiana 70053

D.J. AND THE JAZZ FEST

"D.J., would you like to go to the Jazz Fest this week-end?" asked Mom on our way home from school one day.

"Is it like the fair we have at school, with rides, games, hot dogs, and cotton candy?"

"Oh, it's nothing like that," said Mom. "The Jazz Fest is a festival that New Orleans has every spring. People come from all over to listen to the music. Our city is known as the birthplace of jazz. A New Orleans trumpet player named Buddy Bolden was one of the first musicians to play jazz."

"What's so special about jazz? Does St. Augustine's band play it?"

Mom laughed and said that jazz is special because of how well it expresses feelings. She said that the Jazz Festival is a good way to learn about all types of music, and that music helps us to celebrate life.

Sometimes Mom thinks of boring things for me to do—like going to the Jazz Fest!

Mom made plans for the festival. She invited her godmother, Nanan, to come because she enjoys gospel music.

The weather was great that weekend. Mom said we should wear comfortable shoes and bring hats to help block the sun. I wore my favorite baseball cap and my new sunglasses. I thought I looked cool.

"Do they sell toys here?" I asked as we went into a crafts booth.

"Yes, but the toys here are handcrafted," said Mom.

"What does handcrafted mean?" I asked.

"It means that something was made by hand, not by a factory or store. People like handmade items because they're one of a kind. For example, a handcarved boat is valued more than one bought from a store."

Only Mom would care about that, I thought.

When we got to the Children's Tent, kids were everywhere. Inside the tent there was a stage. Some girls were performing an Oriental dance, using silk scarves. Next to the tent was a make-believe African village and some tables. On the tables were crayons, paint, and paper.

I saw my cousin Jonathan sitting at a table. "Hey, Jonathan, what are you drawing?" I asked.

"My usual thing, D.J.—dinosaurs."

Mom said we should watch the performance in the Children's Tent because there was a karate show going on. There was a boy my size breaking boards with his foot!

How cool, I thought to myself.

Mom joined us and said, "Come on, let's go find Nanan and get something to eat."

The food area at the Jazz Fest was like a big picnic. Everyone sat on the ground to eat. Mom bought Jonathan and me our own shrimp po' boy sandwiches—we didn't even have to split them. Later, we all ate strawberry snowballs to cool off.

We walked back to the gospel tent with Nanan to listen to the choir. The music was so strong, I could feel it passing through my body. I guess that's what Nanan calls the spirit.

People were clapping and waving their hands to the sky. Everyone in the tent started swaying from side to side with the beat of the music. Nanan seemed to be in a trance. Boy, that sure is some powerful music, I thought.

As we walked around the festival, we heard people playing Cajun music with a guitar, an accordion, and a fiddle. Mom saw some people she knew and started dancing.

The music was so lively, you couldn't even tell they were singing in French! By the time the song was over, we were all dancing and twirling around.

Then we passed a blues stage with guitars playing loudly. Mom said it was B. B. King playing the Memphis blues. At another stage, the Neville Brothers were playing the lively sound of Mardi Gras music.

"When I grow up, I'm going to have big muscles like Aaron Neville and play the trumpet in my own band," I said seriously.

Mom laughed and said, "Just don't forget your mother, D.J." Mom thinks of funny things sometimes.

We were almost ready to leave when Mom reminded us to pick
out our treats. Jonathan decided on a handmade drum from an
African booth. The man said it was real. It sure sounded loud.

"What are you getting, D.J.?" asked Jonathan.

"I don't know yet," I said as I walked from booth to booth. I didn't want a top, truck, marbles, or toy boat. I wanted something special. Finally, I saw a booth with butterflies, kites, and flags blowing in the breeze. "That's what I want," I said.

"A kite?" asked Mom.

"No, " I replied, "a flag!"

As we were leaving the Jazz Fest, we heard a loud drum roar. It was St. Augustine's marching band! Mom let us run ahead to catch up with them. Jonathan played his drum and marched next to the drum section. I ran fast to catch up with the flag section at the front of the band.

Mom and Nanan smiled as we marched out proudly with the band. It sure was a great Jazz Fest weekend!